# Jalapeño Bagels

by Natasha Wing
illustrated by Robert Casilla

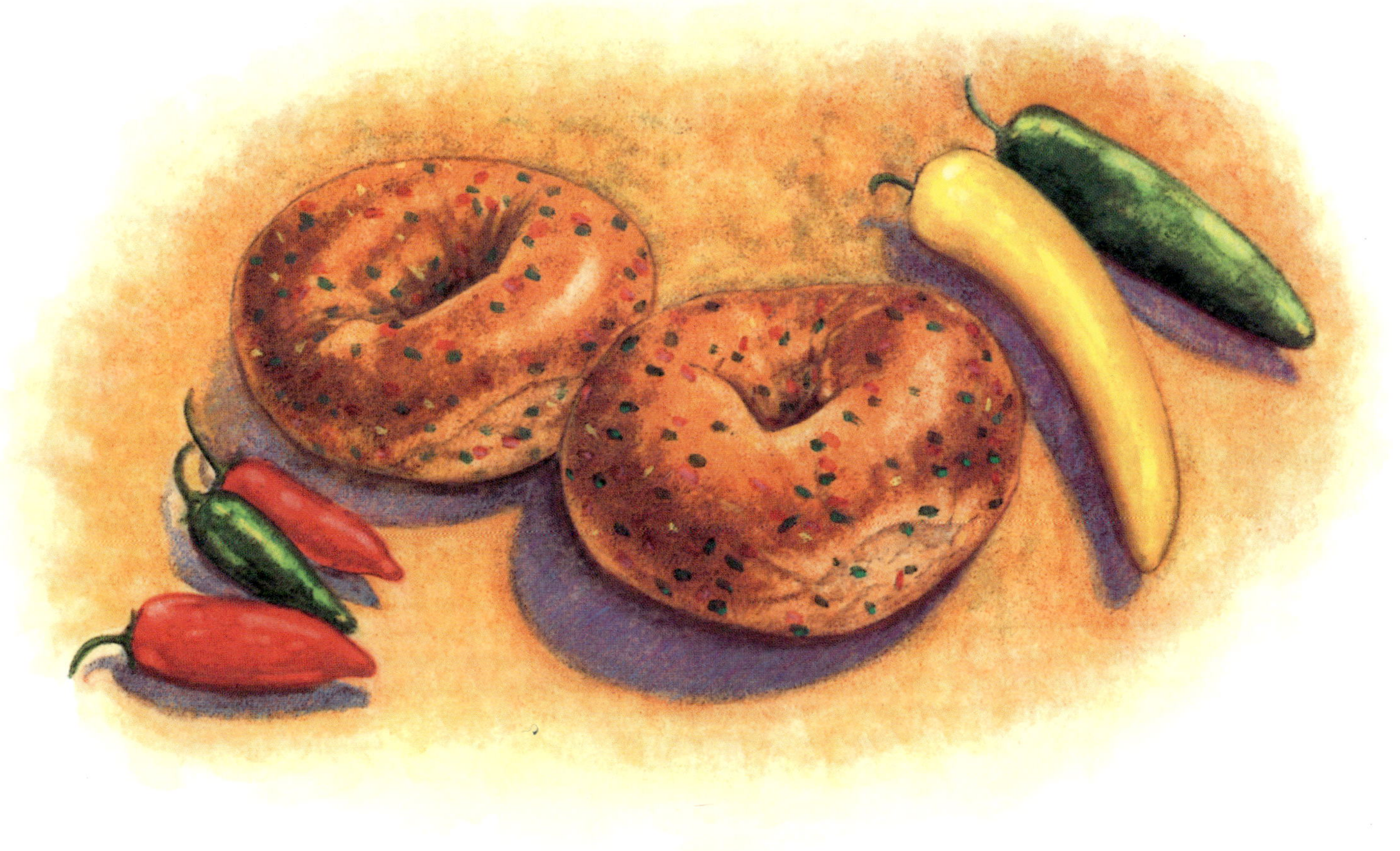

McGraw Hill SRA

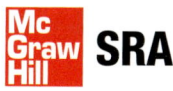

Columbus, OH

"What should I bring to school on Monday for International Day?" I ask my mother. "My teacher told us to bring something from our culture."

"You can bring a treat from the *panaderia,*" she suggests. Panaderia is what Mama calls our bakery. "Help us bake on Sunday—then you can pick out whatever you want."

"It's a deal," I tell her. I like helping at the bakery. It's warm there, and everything smells so good.

Early Sunday morning, when it is still dark, my mother wakes me up.
"Pablo, it's time to go to work," she says.
We walk down the street to the bakery. My father turns on the lights. My mother turns on the ovens. She gets out the pans and ingredients for *pan dulce*. Pan dulce is Mexican sweet bread.
I help my mother mix and knead the dough. She shapes rolls and loaves of bread and slides them into the oven. People tell her she makes the best pan dulce in town.
"Maybe I'll bring pan dulce to school," I tell her.

Next we make *empanadas de calabaza*—pumpkin turnovers. I'm in charge of spooning the pumpkin filling. Mama folds the dough in half and presses the edges with a fork. She bakes them until they are flaky and golden brown. Some customers come to our bakery just for her turnovers.

"Maybe I'll bring empanadas de calabaza instead."

"You'll figure it out," she says. "Ready to make *chango* bars?" Chango means "monkey man."

Mama lets me pour in the chocolate chips and nuts. When she's not looking, I pour in more chocolate chips.

"I could bring chango bars. They're my favorite dessert."

"Mine, too," says Mama. "This batch should be especially good. I put in extra chips."

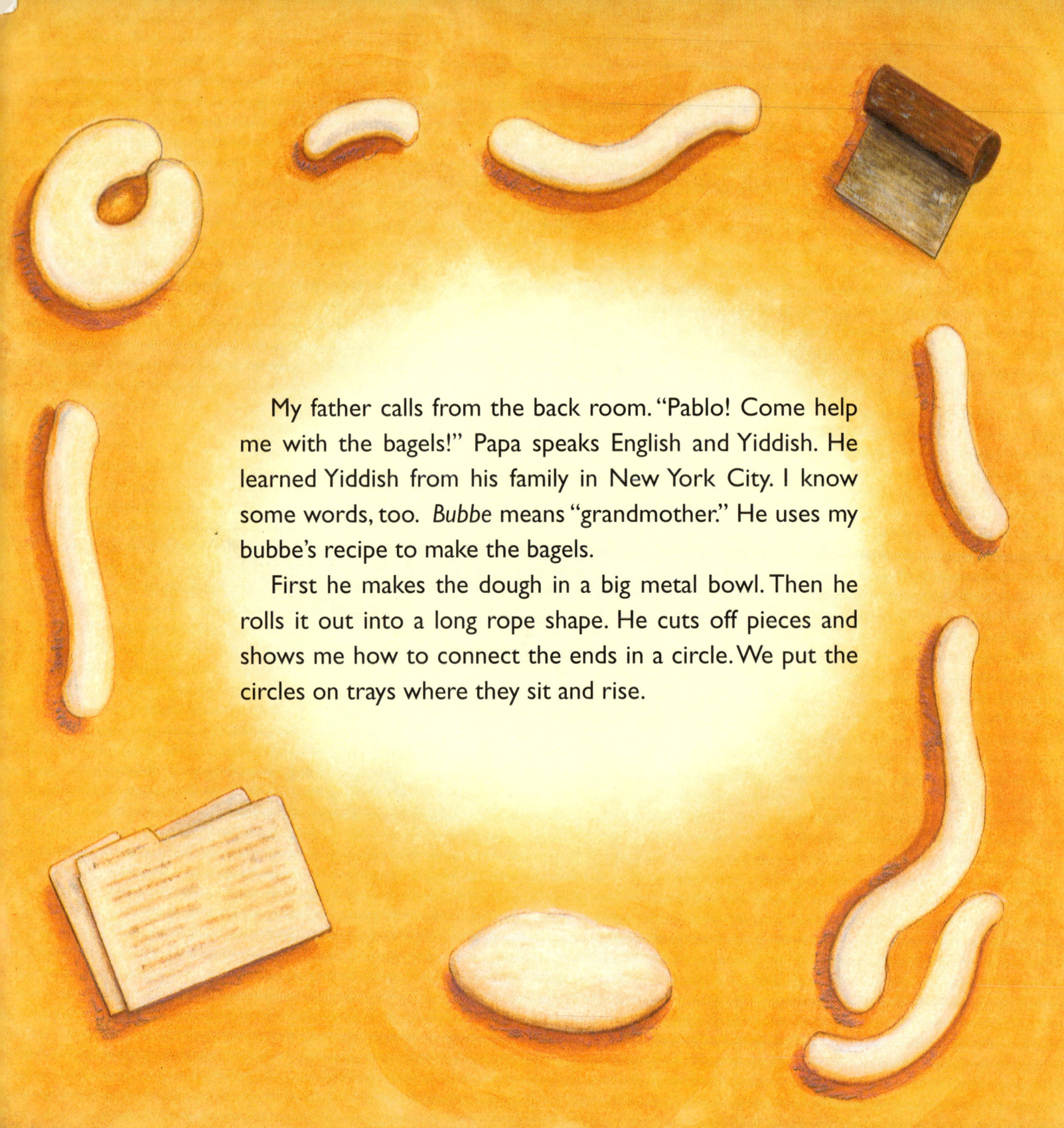

My father calls from the back room. "Pablo! Come help me with the bagels!" Papa speaks English and Yiddish. He learned Yiddish from his family in New York City. I know some words, too. *Bubbe* means "grandmother." He uses my bubbe's recipe to make the bagels.

First he makes the dough in a big metal bowl. Then he rolls it out into a long rope shape. He cuts off pieces and shows me how to connect the ends in a circle. We put the circles on trays where they sit and rise.

While we are waiting my father makes *challah*, Jewish braided bread. He lets me practice braiding challah dough at my own counter. It's a lot like braiding hair. The customers say it is almost too beautiful to eat.

"Maybe I'll bring a loaf of challah to school," I tell Papa. He smiles.

When the bagel dough has risen, he boils the bagels in a huge pot of water and fishes them out with a long slotted spoon. I sprinkle on poppy seeds and sesame seeds, and then they go in the oven.

"Maybe I could bring sesame-seed bagels with cream cheese."

"No *lox*?" Lox is smoked salmon. My father's favorite bagel is pumpernickel with a smear of cream cheese and lox.

I crinkle my nose. "Lox tastes like fish. Jam is better."

My mother joins us and helps my father make another batch of bagels—*jalapeño* bagels. My parents use their own special recipe. While Papa kneads the dough, Mama chops the jalapeño *chiles*. She tosses them into the dough and adds dried red peppers. We roll, cut, make circles, and let them rise. I can't wait until they are done because I am getting hungry.

"Have you decided what you're going to bring to school?" asks Mama.

"It's hard to choose. Everything is so good," I tell her. "I look at Papa. "Except for lox."

"You should decide before we open," warns Mama, "or else our customers will buy everything up."

I walk past all the sweet breads, chango bars, and bagels.

I think about my mother and my father and all the different things they make in the bakery.

And suddenly I know exactly what I'm going to bring.
"Jalapeño bagels," I tell my parents. "And I'll spread them with cream cheese and jam."

"Why jalapeño bagels?" asks Papa.
"Because they are a mixture of both of you. Just like me!"

These recipes are from a real Mexican-Jewish-American bakery, Los Bagels Bakery & Café, in Arcata, California. Kids should ask grown-ups for help with both recipes.

### Chango Bars

½ cup butter
½ cup margarine
2 cups brown sugar
3 eggs
2 1/3 cups flour

1 tablespoon baking powder
1 teaspoon salt
1 cup chocolate chips
1 cup mixed nuts

Melt butter and margarine. While this is melting, cream brown sugar and eggs, then add melted butter and margarine. Combine flour, baking powder, and salt and stir into sugar mixture. Fold in chocolate chips and nuts. Pour mixture into greased 9 inch x 13 inch baking pan and bake 45 to 50 minutes at 350 degrees.

For this recipe you will need lots of time.
But these bagels are worth the wait!

### Jalapeño Bagels

1 ¾ cups lukewarm water
½ teaspoon dry yeast
2 teaspoons salt
1 ½ tablespoons sugar
5 to 6 cups flour
⅓ cup jalapeños, chopped
¼ cup dried red peppers

Mix water, yeast, salt, and sugar. Add flour and jalapeños and mix into a ball. Knead for 10 to 12 minutes, adding more flour if necessary, until dough is stiff. Add red peppers and knead for 3 minutes. Let dough rest 10 minutes, then cut into 12 pieces with a knife.

Roll each piece of dough on a table to form long cigarlike shapes. Then, for each of the twelve pieces, connect the two ends by overlapping them about ¾ of an inch and rolling the ends together to make a ring shape. Make sure each joint is secure or it will come apart while boiling.

Cover with a damp towel and let rise 1 to 1 ½ hours in a warm spot. In a large pot, bring 1 to 2 gallons of water to a rolling boil. Place bagels in boiling water and boil until they float (15 to 30 seconds). Remove with a slotted spoon and place on a lightly greased cookie sheet. Bake at 400 degrees for 10 to 15 minutes or until golden brown.

Note: a bakery uses dry malt instead of sugar, and high-gluten flour, which you may be able to get at a bakery or pizza parlor. For a milder bagel, reduce the quantities of the peppers.

Recipes from *Los Bagels Recipes and Lore* (Arcata, CA: Creative Type, 1991). Copyright © 1991 by Los Bagels. Reprinted with permission.

# GLOSSARY

## Spanish

**chango** (CHAN go) *slang* monkey man
**empanadas de calabaza** (em pa NA das de ka la BA sa) pumpkin turnovers
**jalapeño chiles** (ha la PEN yo CHI les) small, very hot peppers named for Jalapa, the capital of Veracruz
**panaderia** (pa na de RI a) bakery
**pan dulce** (pan DUL se) Mexican sweet breads, which include rolls, bread loaves, cakes, and cookies

## Yiddish

**bagel** (BA gel) leavened, doughnut-shaped hard roll. In Yiddish it is spelled *beygel*.
**bubbe** or **bobe** (BU bee) grandmother
**challah** (KHA la or HA la) Jewish braided bread prepared especially for the Jewish Sabbath. Sabbath falls on the seventh day of the week, Saturday, and is a day of rest and religious observance.
**lox** (loks) smoked salmon that is sliced thin. In Yiddish it is spelled *laks*.

*To Los Bagels, Lender's Bagels, mis amigos,
and my bagel buddy, Dan*
—N.W.

*To the new sugar and spice of my life, Emily.*
—R.C.

From JALAPENO BAGELS by Natasha Wing, illustrated by Robert Casilla. Text Copyright © 1996 by Natasha Wing, Illustrations copyright © 1996 by Robert Casilla. Reprinted by arrangement with Atheneum Books For Young Readers, and Imprint of Simon & Schuster Children's Publishing Division. All rights reserved.

## SRAonline.com

Copyright © 2008 by SRA/McGraw-Hill.

All rights reserved. Except as permitted under the United States Copyright Act, no part of this publication may be reproduced or distributed in any form or by any means, or stored in a database or retrieval system, without the prior written permission of the publisher, unless otherwise indicated.

Printed in Mexico.

Send all inquiries to:
SRA/McGraw-Hill
4400 Easton Commons
Columbus, OH 43219-6188

ISBN: 978-0-07-612493-0
MHID: 0-07-612493-2

2 3 4 5 6 7 RRM 13 12 11 10 09

The **McGraw·Hill** Companies